Rowing Across the Dark

Rowing Across the Dark

POEMS BY
FRANZ DOUSKEY

The University of Georgia Press
Athens, Georgia

Copyright © 1981 by the University of Georgia Press
Athens, Georgia 30602

Set in 10 on 12 point Monticello type
Printed in the United States of America

Library of Congress Cataloging in Publication Data

Douskey, Franz.
  Rowing across the dark.

  I. Title.
PS3554.087R6   811'.54   81-1936
ISBN 0-8203-0574-X   AACR2
ISBN 0-8203-0578-2 (pbk.)

The publication of this book is supported by a grant from the National Endowment for the Arts, a federal agency.

Acknowledgments

Acknowledgment is given to the following publications in which poems from this book first appeared.

Abraxas: "Now That You're Leaving"
The Advocate: "Eddie"
Chelsea: "Everything Is Ready," "Inventions"
En Passant: "Night Swim"
For Neruda / For Chile: "Neruda"
The Georgia Review: "The Sleep Collector," "Clear Moonlight"
The Goddard Review: "History of Stars," "I'm Waiting"
The Greenfield Review: "In a Field, North of Alsace"
Inland Boat Series: "Beirut," "Chief Joseph," "Salt," "Crossing Another Year," "All Your Crimes," "The Prince of Arabia," "Sea of Tranquility," "Waiting for Skylab," "Indian Summer," "Advice to Travelers," "Sitting Across From Death"
Kayak: "The Tragedy of Beasts," "Arrival"
Lazarus: "Gold Leaf & All"
Madrona: "Dying Young"
Mazagine: "The Forgotten"
The New Yorker: "Rowing Across the Dark"
The New York Quarterly: "Fifth Anniversary," "Profiles"
Phantasm: "Thin Air," "Revenge"
Poetry Now: "Block Island," "Flying Over Iowa"
Poets of the Desert Southwest: An Anthology: "Wilderness Encircled"
River Bottom Press Broadside: "The Return"
Rolling Stone: "Night," "Freeing the Alphabet," "Going Home"
Southwest: An Anthology: "The Snake"
The Sou'wester: "Buried City in the Desert"
Telephone: "Me Buxtehude the Full Moon and the Cold Ride Home Through Night Woods"
Zahir: "The Crossing"

FOR THE ONE

Contents

Rowing Across the Dark

Beirut

things move quickly here
the roads are mined
they have trucks just to carry
human parts

I miss you   a minute ago
I was smoking and out of the corner
of my eye I thought I saw your head
on my pillow   I guess I'm losing
my mind

death scares me
I've never seen so much of it
bodies on the roads
blood seeps through shirts and blouses
heads leak and mouths eat dirt

and death could come now
while I smoke and listen to music
anyone might be the enemy
it is scary

you should see the faces of the living
worse than the dead

ten years ago it was different
now we are traveling
into something cold and dark

sometimes I think I'll never see you—
if I get shot up
they'll send what's left in an empty glove
waving goodbye like a flag

1

Chief Joseph

had it not been for the telegraph
you would have won

at the auctions they would be
selling white man's weapons and clothing

what would you say now—
cars are named after animals you used to hunt

it's October 4, 1877
your people in the hills
have no food or blankets
soldiers are killing your men
fucking your women
and cutting off their heads
for taxidermists in St. Louis

you say *from where the sun now stands
I will fight no more forever*

but the fighting goes on
it stretches across the Black Hills
glides over the dark lakes
across the moon in a haze

somewhere in the night
with the drumming of brutal memory
stretched tightly across their hearts
men are preparing to march

Salt

1

slowly
under desert sun
I don't perspire

     I evaporate

salt on my arms
my lips and tongue

I have heard of men
who survive cave-ins
drinking their own urine

maybe time in a cool dark mine
makes urine less salty
but here it's different—
I'm a brown flame walking

my throat is starting to swell

I haven't mentioned the coyotes
still echoing—
I was delirious   I imagined
Apaches in the cliffs
I saw mica arrowheads
arcing like tossed cigarettes

but that was last night

now I must find water

before I crystalize into a pillar
of potassium chloride

2

salt salt
tongue thickening

in a mirage
I see Babylonian fountains
undulating milk baths
women beautifying themselves
men with paunches
but it fades into the sky
and the sun beats down
like a massive laser

cloud way off
empty of rain

desert empty of animals
who come out at night
or pace madly in zoos

3

this seems a good place
as any to die
nothing sudden here

sand and more sand
and a half-protruding
skull of a steer
with its memory eaten clean

4

another night I will either
go crazy or not care

if for a moment I wake up
someone whispers
you will survive
that will be enough

if I make it
and ever want to die
I will keep this place in mind

Rowing Across the Dark

my morphined father
spent the Depression
holed up in a hotel
trying to become a writer
but ended up spending forty years
climbing ladders
and at the top he took out
his paintbrush and painted
church steeples and water tanks

count the winter nights
he'd come home hands numb
his gaunt face frozen
afraid to say he'd been laid off

tonight in morphine dreams
he rows across the dark
where he lowers his line
and while the black lake licks
the sides of his solitary boat
an eight-pound rainbow trout
slaps through the air
glistening in moonlight
silver hook flashing through its upper lip

my father so far under
he doesn't feel a thing

The Tragedy of Beasts

some people get money in the mail.
flowers at the door. champagne evenings.
some men know how to do everything,
right down to smelling the cork.

others arrive in the middle of the night
buttons missing,
needing a place to stay.

I've large hands that never know what to do.

some men know the vintage years
and rinse their mouths with chilled wine.
their smiles are made of tiny bones.

others can't get a job
or make love because of the bruises.

it's an old story told again and again
we think will happen to someone else.
it's an old story we never believe
until it follows us and becomes our story,
the tragedy of beasts
who can hold everything but love.

Crossing Another Year

1

three parties
and I'll go to one
but it's hard to dance
when it's another year gone

I'm almost forty
the miracles don't last

each year I make it to autumn
I travel less
I get so cold inside
I close off the rooms

oh lucky professors in California
not to drive on highways hidden with ice

if insurance companies
tied a meter to our hearts
the needle would go off the scale

2

every winter   every fear

my father's face thins
my mother shrinks
my sister dyes her hair
and I cough while making love

now most depressing night of the year
the parties and tv going
frustrations sucked out of bottles

I'm hoping I was sent to this planet
to make love and risk disaster
and any minute I'll be taken back

All Your Crimes

tell me again
about the hard choices
the people out to get you
imaginary affairs
how you survived the death camps
of universities and skid row
the anguished phone calls
the shadows that won't go away
the standing ovation
in the unemployment line
when you told them to shove it
the college girls who scream
when you show up in your raincoat
the drunken beds in forgotten rooms
with broken venetian blinds
and the loans that will never be paid

but you leave scars
wounded self-history
a life of crime
whose only victim
walks unseen inside you

The Prince of Arabia

I am the Prince of Arabia
the one known for his golden peacock
his harem of Skidmore runaways
his purity of soul and luminous meditations

I can conjure up anything
a waterfall leaping through a hoop
fireproof volcanoes
clouds filled with oarsmen
a pillar of salt turning into a woman

I can press a revolver to my lips
and resist hooks that are lowered from the sky
I greet every tortuous deception
with an impervious smile

I can thrive in downpours and in careless pleasures
but I can't do anything about the night

an avalanche of coal down a narrowing tunnel

Sea of Tranquility

FOR DAVID

here I come
life-support system on my back
crawling down the ladder

I look toward earth
and see it glowing
shopping centers lit for Christmas

I have brought a 12-year-old girl
wearing pink pajamas

on earth every desire is criminal
but there are no laws here
not even the one of gravity
no such thing as a bad habit

here the morning sun splits open
it almost came too late for me

I take off my shirt
it stays air-borne
. . . . my flag

tell them it's so easy to be happy
I no longer lack belief

don't expect to write for awhile

Waiting for Skylab

my wife has gone to New Hampshire.

she heard we are in the path,
a small, Victorian house
that has survived hurricanes,
floods and generations of carpenter ants.

she has left the tomatoes,
still green and tied like hostages.
she has left her music students,
future geniuses stunted by the advance
of a space craft that was launched
before most of them were born.

their mothers call;
I tell them the truth.

my wife has gone to New Hampshire
and will return Thursday or Friday,
or after the rain of nuts and bolts,
cameras and tangled gyroscopes
have eaten our roof like satanic moths.

right now I'm in the parlor
reading the morning paper.
I follow all the predictions
and scientific calculations
calm in the knowledge that nothing
spectacular will happen to me.

Indian Summer

this is the last Sunday
before we reverse our clocks
the last night before the first freeze

I can smell winter
in the dead leaves and wood smoke

tomorrow the sun will shine
the color of dirty gauze

winter's wild mouth will be everywhere

Advice to Travelers

the gypsies told me
about this place

windows lit in kerosene light
dust rising from the roads

the people here eat black meat
the dead pause and then go on

and not far away
there is a hill

you can see sand whirling from planets
and the stars hang down like embers
the ocean is endlessly tied to the same shore

in the winter
roofs are covered with soot
the windows are hidden behind snowdrifts

in the town square there is a flag
with a charred crucifix
in honor of those who live
proliferating darkness

there are several places that welcome
houseguests and two restaurants
accept all major credit cards
but it's recommended that you drive right through

Sitting Across From Death

at a reunion dinner
the woman across from me smiles
and drops a pill into my wine glass

soon everyone is purple
their eye muscles
fill the room with twitches

I leave the table
the woman follows me into the garden

she wears a black lace choker
like an orbit of death around her neck

I'm afraid to look into her eyes
so deep I might never come out

she says *you have to know what you want*
before you can know who you are
then she undresses slowly

in the garden
there's a pool with no bottom
surrounded by gypsy moss

stars spark like feldspar

we kiss and she is cold
I'm afraid she'll push me into the pool
clutch me as we sink in endless water

when I open my eyes she is someone else
she has to go home to her fiancé
take off her black choker
and let him kiss the cool fringes of her neck

I watch her walk toward town
under a railroad bridge
then I go back inside

someone sitting next to me
tells me what a great dinner I've missed

Gate's Pass

six years ago we ran bare-foot
through the desert

we weren't afraid of gila monsters
jumping cholla or diamondbacks

we raced each other
and the first one to the top
became silent look-out

hundreds of feet below
cars moved slowly
tourists posed in front of the ramada
and took pictures of the Arizona sunset

one July afternoon
we saw a double rainbow

what we remember travels with us
and what we forget stays where we leave it
like names dropped into hermetic night

we find others as we stumble across them
and they glow inside for the rest of our lives

Dying Young

I no longer have the option of dying young

—RICHARD SHELTON

at a certain point
skin begins to hang like sackcloth
and friends who haven't killed themselves
left their lovers or married for better or worse
have grown torpid dreaming of what might have been

in the middle of this I rise
not like a Phoenix
but like a mocking bird

death I say
kiss my ass

dying young is one option I can do without

Thin Air

the horizon darkens and keeps on going

good air at a premium
you better save your breath for the soup
or when your heart is shell-struck
and you're in the thick of it without a mask

January February sucking and jerking
try getting a quarter from everyone
ask for lemonade and you get a cigarette

crawl forward unable to resist
it's not all apple sauce
gentleness

shake your head if you want
lie face down
heavenly bodies a big success
but here on earth we didn't leave much

strangest of all is the promptness of garbage trucks
the poetic faces of two workers
our beautiful fertile earthy bits and pieces

Hidden Fear

love, what is there
we try to make last?

we rub it smooth,

then we wake up miles
from where we fell asleep.

Block Island

we arrive
open our suitcases

in the next room honeymooners
try to resolve some unspent desire
and their bed almost bangs through the wall

you and I take a long bike ride
to the cliffs where the Narragansetts
drove the Mohegans into the ocean

in a few hours we get back to the inn
the honeymooners are still going at it

the moon comes up
the honeymooners continue
and I wonder when the Narragansetts
drove the Mohegans over the cliffs
did they yelp and howl like honeymooners
beat their drums like the honeymooners
beat their bed against the wall

and when it was over did the Narragansetts
look down to the bloodied Mohegans
who lay at the bottom of the cliff
and whisper *was it good for you too*

Night Swim

I go down and come up.
you are knee-deep;
nipples shiny as bullets.

after five years,
we are new.

in nights illuminated
by invariable memory
we keep love burning.

in a world let loose of love
we stay with what we know
and grow where we are planted.

Fifth Anniversary

we don't stand together
patting each other on the back.
if we have anything to say,
we say it quietly.

we go to bed early;
we have so much faith we don't pray.

if we remember anything,
we remember our innocence.
if we forget anything,
it's how the scars got there.

if we have any questions,
we save them for later.
if we need anything in the night,
we close our eyes and hope it goes away.

if we have desire,
we are thankful,
even when it arrives chipped and scarred.

if we cry,
we do it alone,
when it's too late.

if we want solitude,
we spit words between our teeth like knives.

if we want a kiss,
we ask for something else;
if we want something else,
we kiss.

if we learn anything,
it's to laugh whenever we can,
and if we get drunk,
we climb the stairs one at a time.

if we commit crimes,
we never know how long we have
before we are discovered;
if we tell lies,
we never know which ones
we will be forced to live.

if we stop breathing,
the night shines through us.
if we close our eyes,
we are trunks of dark trees.

if we find God,
we find half-melted snow.

if we touch each other,
we discover Atlantis,
Morocco, and Trinidad at sunset.

if we make love,
we revolve on the propellers of ecstasy.

if the light fades,
there is the afterglow.

if there is more,
we are happy.

Passages

One Place to Another

on earth
sullen bodies
lurch toward death.
they could walk by
a wall of bougainvillea
and not see abundant red.

to get along,
agree with everyone;

eat ashes,
pay the phone bill,
answer all those letters
from hell,

laugh at death
and pretend you're not
going crazy with pain.

have your smile ready,
even for the mailman.

Spectral Journey

I wonder why there's so little
joy; no dark woods to get lost in.
locks on everything.

now and then a creature staggers
toward me, face swinging with pain.

eight-year-old children
ask adult questions,
then I find a copy of a local paper.

it tells of suicides,
security and radiation leaks,
children starving to death,
quarterly profits of the multi-nationals,
the pulsating price of daily bread
and my horoscope for tomorrow.

Forgotten Province

I follow railroad tracks
that arrive at a river bank,
then sink into thick, green water.

trees have artificial limbs.

telepathic birds zero in,
and on the breath of dying leaves
I can smell blood.

Accommodations

one body per person:
teeth, bones, brain,
liver, sexual organs,
not necessarily used in that order.

my body is fine;
I can sit down,
have brain storms,
and get up and leave.

once a week love is brought in
on a platter.
suddenly it's impossible
to speak the truth,

and then another week passes.

Going Through the Door

old habits make me want you.
it's midnight, five hours before
I leave your warm room
and catch the *Montrealer.*

you say you're tired
some other time

I turn from your mouth,
another murky death
under the catastrophe of the moon.

Sixth Movement

to die is a horrible thing,
but to not live is worse.

all our beautiful minds are twisted inward,
inhabitants of trees are made extinct,
and the only man-made object visible from space
is pollution from the Four Corners
Power Plant, near Farmington, New Mexico.

to watch a woman commit suicide
on tv without changing expression,
to watch children burn to death in tenement fires,

to watch the war in a far away desert
as flies buzz with desire,
and no one asks, "What am I doing to cause pain?
How can I change? What can I give up
so that another's agony is lessened?"

no money spent on starving, abandoned
street-children in Argentina, Mexico,
New York or Calcutta,
but each year billions of dollars are spent
to improve tv reception.

On Living Light

every possession weighs something.
a 250-page novel weighs half a pound.
if you own more than two-hundred books,
a stereo, a tv, a car, silverware, and are
at least 5'2", between the ages
of 21 and 55, you are overweight.

if a man weighs 160 lbs.
and tries to possess two women
whose combined weight is 220 lbs.,
he is overweight.

if a woman tries to free herself
from under the weight of struggle,
she mustn't be afraid of tearing her stockings.

Drawing Together

somewhere,
beyond the dark,
a violin is playing.

the desert turns cold.

if it wasn't for the fire
of dried palm leaves,
dancers in thin veils
making obscene thrusts,
and the lamb rotating on a spit,
I would say your name over and over.

but it's different here.
no one speaks my language,
and I don't speak theirs.

I lie near the fire
and worship its warmth.

I close my eyes and see
radiance after radiance.

Falling Through

the burning light comes back
and touches me.

I'm falling through silent,
snow-filled space.

far below, on earth,
I can hear voices.

up here,
stars are still a mystery;
not solid as I imagined,
but spirals of inaccessible nebula.

clouds are filled with vapors,
doorknobs and eggshells.

when the wind is still,
I hear clouds rub each other,
and when they break apart,
I see the glowing earth
covered by a late-night snowfall.

Coming Home

I've been away two months.
I'm 20 lbs. lighter.
the smell of roasting meat
makes me ill.

the first night we go to bed
you ask *what's the matter?*

I go to the window.
stars are bright, white dots.
I connect them and see
the outline of a bull,
a sword, and a man-horse.

one minute it's impossible
to love, then I look at you
and it's impossible not to.

Alone

now I feel it's time to be
alone,

to sit hushed,
and when you want me,
all you have to do is think;

we've been together that long.

Neruda

they've taken the poet's hand
and chained it to the bed of the ocean
where he dreams of blood

he was standing by the window
looking across the ocean
when the lights went out

when the lights went out
the people pretended to be asleep
but the heart of the poet stopped

the poet dreams of stars
at the bottom of the ocean

the poet's body is empty

if you hold it to your ear
you'll hear the ocean

you'll hear how a man sounds
as his life leaves his body

it's an old song you'll never forget

Me Buxtehude the Full Moon
and the Cold Ride Home Through Night Woods

as I skid maniacally homeward
WQXR is fading in and out like weak anesthetic

the moon is a yellow mouth
rising in the rear-view mirror
while fog and an autumn frost steam the windows

the wipers barely streak an opening—

with one hand jockeying the wheel
and the other wiping the windshield
I turn from one set of ruts
into the muddy hollows of another

QXR is garbled by a station from Montreal
someone's selling Fords in the language of Rimbaud

I park along side the mailbox
then walk through wet witch grass
until I reach the porch

inside the cabin I light a fire in the stove
sit in the cushioned chair and listen
to the wood arch upward in flames
listen to the clock when everything settles
and hear strains of organ music
carried off in ambulances of wind

I get up and slide another chunk of elm onto the fire
and try to think of something to do
something that can be done alone in the half-eaten dark

Tornado

low yellow sky comes toward me
the planet vibrates

nests fence posts a cistern
bales of tangled wire a tractor fender
and a straw hat swirl in yellow dust

the twister's whirling funnel
spits out a splintered barn one board at a time

it roars across the field
sucking the garden and orchard clean

my work jacket ripples
as I lie flat on the road

the tornado passes like a great earth god
tearing up trees and onions
utility poles and beehives

and as it moves on toward Waterloo
I'm not the same man
but one who has kept his ear to the ground
and has heard the awful drumming inside

Everything Is Ready

the rain's on the roof
the whisky's on my tongue
and the cat's in bed
meticulously licking herself

in the loft a bat twitches
he wants the light off

soon he'll be down
circling my head like a lariat

the whisky's making
small holes inside and the rain's
making small holes outside

here we are
man and bat
our shadows on the wall
like cave paintings

the earth pitches forward
and I knock over the lamp

now it's man and bat
circling each other on the ceiling

meanwhile the floor's getting ready—
it's been getting ready a long time

Eddie

you were the strong one
black belt
biceps as big as saucers
and you could hit a baseball
four-hundred feet while your wife
and two blond sons watched
but how do I make sense of the world

while driving Emily home
she tells me you had been tapping maples
with a gas-powered tapper

you noticed something wrong
and when you tried to tap the next tree
the bit shattered and fragments flew into your eyes
and lodged in your brain

while you lay on the ground
your wife hollered at you for abandoning her
she cried for the pain you were going through
then prayed you would die without suffering any longer

I stop the car

I don't believe you're dead
you couldn't have died
you were everything some men dream of being

one defective gas-powered tapper
one the company forgot to recall
the one the hardware store didn't remember selling
has made all the difference in the world

Gold Leaf & All

I got tired of the complaints
too much rain and never enough heat
so I threw the bible into the fire
gold leaf & all

watched it burn as page after page
turned black
the small print vanishing

I left the cabin
and walked through the rain
to my car that won't start in the rain

it didn't start so I walked
back to the cabin
through mud and manure
up the stone steps

onto the rotting porch
through the doorway
and over to the fire

the good book was smoldering
I turned it over
and it caught nicely

page after page
curling like a widow's shawl

Inventions

he came to me
asking why I'd forsaken him

poor creature
I did what I could

I said *you can be my God*
no one will know the difference

he shivered in a corner of himself
biting his nails and doubting me

I lowered my knees to the dirt
cooing his small name
to see if he'd come

this frightened him
he ran out the door
saying he'd return

so now I know about him
and what hungers after me
when the fire suckles wood
and the begging wind comes up
over the world like a sickle

Now That You're Leaving

now that you're leaving
my life will be better

I'll bite into a pear with no worm
get a haircut
and look out the window

twenty-one and you're leaving
for older ruins
to live on a coffee plantation
and hide your money in your left boot

you'll be gone one month
maybe two your crucifix will wear out

you'll miss your mascara

some night
when the floor has got you dizzy
the refrigerator will click on
2,000 miles away

I'll wake up
and know you were right

The Return

old cabin that kept me warm
during July floods when neighbors
gathered by the river and watched
the covered bridge survive the swollen waters

and the holy tree with bushy brain
that kept me cool during August
when the corn that endured the flood withered
and locusts filled the bright air with a tedious buzz

I'm home again

I dance on the rain wet road
and breathe like a man discovering
air

something glimmers in the roadside gravel
I bend and see a firefly whose bulb is nearly burnt out

I watch the small light in this total
fog-filled darkness then I go

turn the key in the rusted padlock
walk into the cabin
and smell the must that mice
and no one living here has made

I close the door
strike a match and the cabin
fills with shadows—

old friends who welcome me
and I don't move for a long time

41

Remembering the Lost

the lost don't vanish like footsteps down the hall
they inhabit dark places and haunt us
because of crimes no one remembers

if we pretend they don't exist
we carry them inside forever
if we ask them to leave
we find them waiting for us everywhere

whatever door opens we wander through
and in the dark an old memory comes toward us
tapping its cane

fear flies through us like sparks from a grinding wheel

we wonder how we could have forgotten
the dislocated fear rearing beneath the streetlight
the old wound if ever healed would make us free/destroy us

What the Hell Is Going On, Really

last night migratory dream travelers
flew over-head in bowling pin formation.
virgins dressed in snakeskins
were selling hibernating corpses door to door.
then the moon came up, and I could see
the E-Z Method Driving School training car
spinning its wheels in a snowbank.

an Arab, driving an oil truck,
parked in front of my house.
I went out and found
the mailman in the hallway
blown up by a letter from Ireland.

I went back inside,
and there were two porpoises
making love on my waterbed.

I called the police.
they said they couldn't come;
they had to remain neutral
until a crime had been committed.

I lit a fire in the fireplace;
tiny creatures crawled out of the woodwork
and began to dance in the flames.

one giant, drunk moth
kept bumping his head against the picture window;
he was collecting for mute, halt and blind moths.

I opened the door and he flew into the fire.

I don't know which lasted longer,
the crackling of his fiery bones
or his wings cutting into the night like lighter fluid.

Arrival

ah
here I come
now with my cadillac
whistle down the dark
streets with as many face
as there are windows

here
I come
rounding the corner
in my best suit

approaching the old
pain with a new set
of keys and all of them fit

Profiles

The Literary Genius

he writes about his friends
turning against him,
about war and being drunk
and what a pain in the ass
his old lady is.

he writes about being 48,
pot-bellied and how he suffers
because the New York poets
have it in for him.

he writes about revenge
and about women he could never have.

if he stuck to writing
about what he knows,
he could produce
a book of one page on which
is written a very short haiku.

Someday

I don't believe
you. you laugh at
all the wrong times,
like when I'm in pain,
or when I want to make
love, you laugh; and when
the old lady got drenched

by a passing car, and when
your brother got busted
for possession, you laughed.

someday someone's gonna
cut out your heart
and stuff it in an olive.

Dear Mad Poet

please don't phone
after midnight,
or dance naked outside
my window.

nothing happens accidentally,
or on purpose;
it's all written in the broken stones
in a language we have forgotten.

I wish I could help,
but poetry is Russian
roulette with all the cylinders empty.

the only pleasure I get
is publishing more than my enemies
and giving them addresses
of the poetry schools you have already ruined.

The Critic

isn't there anyone you like?
Chagall is too blue,
Rubinstein is too stiff,

Lartigue was an amateur,
Breughel too primitive
and Stravinsky too strident.

you have Milton's eyes for art
and Van Gogh's ear for music.

Poet on 92nd Street

he's dignified,
signing copies of his books,
pretending life's always been this way,
but there were times
his pants were so thin
that if he sat on a nickel
he could tell if it was heads or tails.

now the critics say he's lost
his touch. his poems don't have
the fire of his early ones.

when he was a young man no woman
wanted him, but now that he's famous
the women arrive: beautiful, available,
but too late.

he's so cold that butter
won't melt in his mouth.

somewhere in his childhood
he must have signed a contract
guaranteeing that he would always be unhappy.

Flying Over Iowa

31,000 feet below
five roads join like a star.

this isn't much to report,
but with snowy flatlands to the horizon
five roads joining is a major event.

occasionally a rill of dark earth
snakes across a field
as though a giant mole has passed underneath.

up here,
immense sky;
and down there,
endless earth.

it's hard to imagine
one God for all this,

much less one president.

Cambodian Temple Rubbing

three male warriors stand
with right legs poised in the air.
in their left hands they hold bows
with no bow strings.

they wear pointed hats and crocodile
tails to frighten the game.

each warrior faces west, smiling.
there are no clouds behind them,
no sky.

these rubbings are rare;

years after the bombings
there are no temples.

In a Field, North of Alsace, June 23, 1915

just as we expected,
the dark figure of a farmer
is suddenly lit by lightning.

fully rational, despite loss of blood,
there's no returning,
but we don't cry out.

so tired. . . . so tired.
our bodies are strange,
broken vicissitudes of instinct.

once, when crossing the river,
we were all crazy,
temporarily transcending our conflicts.

some of us had been tortured, burned,
stopped by bullets while professing religions.

we could see horses and packmules,
glimpses of heaven,
accumulated sins encamped in human thickets.

foundering and protesting,
we're not frightening any longer.

we fill with smoke and blacken
like bundles in a field on a shadowless night.

The Sleep Collector

he comes at night
and says *dream on*
but it's no use

I had a snake doctor
who told me *burn your crops*
recite backwards the unaccountable solitudes
and remember the nights inhabited by clamoring parakeets

impossible horrors swoop in slow motion
and mate in the rafters in bat dung

he said *remember the unmissed immovable beings*
who became clearer after midnight
and like wild tapeworms have no voices

night after night the same fear spirals in
and I imagine stars are the eyes of angry crows

if I arrive before dark
I'm safe from shadowy motions
from menacing inevitabilities and their admirable disguises

I'm immune to death clacking across tiles
and the blond uncomprehending silence that encourages it

Night

time to sleep by the fire
dream of blue lanterns
trailing across the Pacific

History of Stars

you can't hear them.
want to see the extent of the damage?
look into their eyes.
when they blink
a great door closes behind them.

many turn cold,
lose their grip on the vast black sea.

lovers in parked cars divide them,
repeat *I want you* in the warm, soaked night,
only to return to silence.

accidental kisses interpreted
as though stars belong to us
because we bend them to our uses.

try to sing them to sleep,
bed them down among drunken shadows,
live like you mean it.

bear up those small birds you wear for eyes;
look among the snapshots of the missing.
everywhere stars are burning luxuriously,
and the night continues more or less invisible.

Clear Moonlight

the moon is not so innocent
one eye looking through a keyhole
opulent in all that darkness
going beyond my blackest thoughts

this is the hour blue nipples appear
inviolate knowledge descends
and enters backward into an empty house

lovers along the canal
report mysterious floating objects
and rivers run from their beds

everywhere blood is on fire
some of us place bets on prayer wheels
others hide under the covers and deny everything

we hump a little pain
and wake up the next morning clear

each day is as tedious as a needle
in search of slivers under the skin

everyone is well-balanced
no madness no hope no desire
not too much salt no white shoulders of the moon
and nothing invisible to believe in

The Snake

in daylight the snake
with his iridescent simplicity
curls up on a smooth flat rock

when in the distance
he hears infant mice cry out
his scales stampede toward fulfillment
he flicks his tongue
says *sshhh*

his colors crackle over leaves
hypnotic hairpinned body straightens
and layer after layer merges with the earth

eyes trained perfectly
his body stretches
then a snap a transfusion
and the air sucks with death

blue night slumps over the hills
the snake is asleep
a caravan of mice pass through him
going home in cold baffling darkness

Revenge

FOR L.W.H.

sometimes it's better to be a zombie
than to admit the feelings I don't want to own

rather than let the anger out
it burns until I have the sick feeling
I'm going to kill the next person through the door

if I could get drunk
I'd drink until I see pulsing white spots

I'd go to the mirror and see myself grinning stupidly
and I'd walk from room to room
trying to think good thoughts

if I'm lucky the liquor
hits like a dropped anvil
and I stumble from leg to leg to bed

I lie there
ferried through the dark
shivering as I grab the sheets

I float in and out of cold dreams
amazed famished rocking with laughter

fat thighs sever my head like scissors
and traces of perfume stifle but never mind

it's an old dream that eats me slowly

every night at this time it begins
and there's nothing anyone without love can do

I'm Waiting

all the tears have gathered
like forgotten childhood treasures
as anonymous as badly frightened passersby.

oh maybe I'll go west;
they have better nightmares there.

you get a room, lock the door;
you don't even have to go to bed.
sinister sucking sounds inside the walls;
a sudden dryness crushes your mouth;
you might as well throw all your books away.

you name it:
the sheets drying their blood;
insect antennae signaling
like complicated electronic equipment.

all right, just close your eyes;
spiders with delicate legs drop down.

well, that's not for me.
I keep my eyes open like astral cabbages;
I bring in an extra chair.

sleep, I say, *sit down,*
have a pipe dream,
seduce me.

Freeing the Alphabet

Nothing Remains

when I finish with the rooster
his crown is a crushed sunset

a tablespoon of blood
becomes honey

Beginning to Disappear

my foot is a root
the rest is disappearing

a rusty smile

a mouth full of onion soup

Winter in Fairbanks

when it's forty below
exhale

your breath crystallizes
hovers in the air in a cluster

the natives call this
a *star whisper*

Things Happen

give into temptation
do it nobly

misfortunes arrive daily
separately

call it keeping in touch

The Nipple as a Moving Target

the mouth a little fever
the teeth a bunch of bones that won't crush

I keep raising the wrong vital organ

Uneasiness Returns

I'm at dinner
everyone eats mushrooms
and talks Buddhism

they forget (or don't know)
Buddha died eating mushrooms

The Door Won't

I find a brain in a milk bottle
delivered accidentally (?)

the brain is frozen
monstrous thoughts rise like heavy cream

they spill into the room
and the door won't

close

The Circle Dance

I make love with
the right half
of my brain

in the left half
poisons collect

then you walk in
and I start over

Liquid Tiger

I rub it into my third eye
and go up into the mountains

a strange thing happens—
stars are quarreling like bees
and an old piece of meat on the roadside
keeps yelling *My thumb My Thumb*

The Forgotten

I had hoped to live
as one who breathes the purest air
and is delivered by furious kisses

I anticipate joy
sensual surrenders in glistening groves
but the road darkens and narrows

above shivering gardens stars freeze and break apart

surrounded by silence and inextinguishable desire
I think of other men who at age fourteen
knew exactly what their life's work would be

if there is a god who watches over
those of us who make up our minds at thirty-six
I keep the sliding door open
I keep the coffee warm

I keep my eyes open
and celebrate the homecoming of night

In the Night

in the night,
when you open your ration box of kisses,
don't ask the lips, *what part are you from?*

lower your mysterious hair
and let me kiss your mouth's dark cargo.

blue eyes,
goblets of ocean,
when you peel the layers of mirror back,
bend over me.

bring down your hair like fishermen
bring in their nets in the fire
glow of night full of sensual fishes.

Nipples

your nipples
are two beehives
beehives that breathe

your nipples
are two lozenges
stuck to the outside of their packages

are thimbles too small
for the thumbs inside your breasts
are hats with pink brims

raspberries

two erasers
that erase all the anger in me

Buried City in the Desert

near the mesa,
under what were adobe walls,
we find a buried city.

in white moonlight
we discover bones, pottery,
woven fabrics and turquoise.

in a room that must have been
the Kiva of the priests
we find sandals, a flute
and ancient markings in gold.

when the wind blows through
what were windows
it sounds like a flute.

we are so close to the spirits
we don't move or speak.

through the hole in the roof
the moon pours in like a searchlight;
we see snakes twisting across our boots.

we leave the bones and turquoise untouched.
we climb out of the Kiva
and drive silently to Santa Fe.

four years later
we meet in Manhattan,
and over cocktails we talk

about Tucson, Taos, Mazatlan,
but not once do we mention
the buried city in the desert;

we know we are still on Indian land.

Wilderness Encircled

the woods the woods
we're killing them

some nights they run through themselves
like wildmen with their hair on fire

don't follow me
I've left everything behind
it's your burden now

I leave false clues
a broken hedge
steps leading to the meadow
road signs reversed

I can't be trusted with a lie
and see only when darkness
is waved in front of me

go away
there's enough to haunt us
without searching for ghosts

don't let the bulldozers
disturb your sleep

be careful of the flame
that runs from the river—

wait for me there

Going Home

this place exists
in my imagination

if I start out now
I'll reach it

it'll be desert dark
beyond where all roads end

elf owl and coyote
harmonizing

The Crossing

1

another year thins into winter
this one no different from the rest
the world series has been decided
the awards have been given out

this year's sacrificial poet
along with this year's sacrificial rock star
and this year's sacrificial comedian
have all died while the earth was warm

it was the year of the coldest winter in history
the year of the hottest summer
the year of the drought followed by floods
and the year more criminals than ever
took their group therapy to the streets

it was the year rust started to scar our fenders
it was the year we threw away our vows and remarried
it was the year we played tennis
jogged rode our bikes bought mo-peds
and still grew older

2

I have cut the last of the wood
and piled it on the front porch
to let winter know I'm ready

now I sit in the sun for the last time
this year's last bee hums along my knuckles
this year's last leaves yellow and fall
this year's first chimney smoke rises
storm windows are washed and set into place

this year's quietest Saturday goes unnoticed

3

I have crossed the river of days
and the rapids of months
in the small boat of one year

the moles have all gone home
the geese have formed a wedge and flown south
the sun angles toward Peru
the wind blows through a dark corridor from up north
old friends leave and their children return home

the year is over
and some of us missed it entirely